**SCHOLASTIC**
# News
**Nonfiction Readers**

D0175927

# Uranus

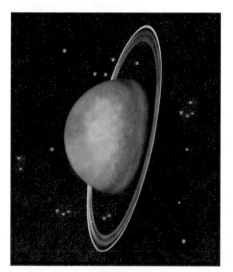

## by
## Christine Taylor-Butler

SCHOLASTIC INC.

New York  Toronto  London  Auckland  Sydney
Mexico City  New Delhi  Hong Kong  Buenos Aires

These content vocabulary word builders
are for grades 1-2.

Consultants: Daniel D. Kelson, Ph.D.
Carnegie Observatories
Pasadena, CA
and
Andrew Fraknoi
Astronomy Department, Foothill College

Photo Credits:

Photographs © 2005: AP/Wide World Photos: cover; Getty Images/Antonio M. Rosario/The Image Bank: 5 top left, 9; NASA: back cover, 1, 2, 4 top, 4 bottom right, 5 bottom, 7, 13, 15, 17, 19, 23 right; Photo Researchers, NY/Detlev van Ravenswaay: 4 bottom left; PhotoDisc/Getty Images via SODA: 23 left. Illustration on page 5 and 11 by Pat Rasch Diagram on pages 20-21 by Greg Harris

Book Design: Simonsays Design!

ISBN 0-516-25303-4

12 11 10 9 8 7 6 5          6 7 8 9 10/0

Printed in the U.S.A.          08

First Scholastic paperback printing, October 2005

# CONTENTS

# WORD HUNT

Look for these words as you read. They will be in **bold**.

**crater**
(**kray**-tur)

**solar system**
(**soh**-lur **siss**-tuhm)

**Titania**
(tuh-**tane**-yuh)

4

## gas giants
(gass **jye**-uhnts)

## orbit
(**or**-bit)

## Uranus
(**yur**-uh-nus)

## *Voyager 2*
(**voi**-ij-uhr 2)

5

# Uranus!

**Uranus** has an ocean.

Can you swim in the ocean on Uranus?

No, you cannot.

The ocean on Uranus is gas that changed into liquid.

It is very hot.

Uranus is the seventh planet from the Sun.

Uranus, Jupiter, Neptune, and Saturn are the biggest planets in our **solar system**.

Sometimes they are called the **gas giants**.

They are mostly made of gas.

Jupiter

Uranus

Saturn

Neptune

Uranus **orbits** the Sun on its side.

It spins like a wheel.

The other planets in our solar system spin like tops.

Scientists think Uranus was hit by something that tipped it sideways.

Saturn

Mars

Mercury

Venus

Uranus

Sun

Asteroids

Earth
Moon

Neptune

11

Uranus has 11 rings.

They are hard to see.

The rings on Uranus are made of ice. The ice is covered in dark dust.

Uranus has more than 27 moons.

The largest moon is **Titania**.

Titania has **craters**, like Earth's moon.

It also has long, deep marks that stretch around it.

**Uranus and 5 of its moons.**

Miranda is also one of Uranus's moons.

Miranda is one of the oddest worlds anywhere.

It has craters. It has long marks. It has broken rocks. It has giant cliffs.

Scientists know how Miranda got some marks but they do not know about them all.

Miranda

*Voyager 2* is a space probe.

It is the only craft to go near Uranus.

It is why we know more about this planet.

Thank you, *Voyager 2*!

Voyager 2

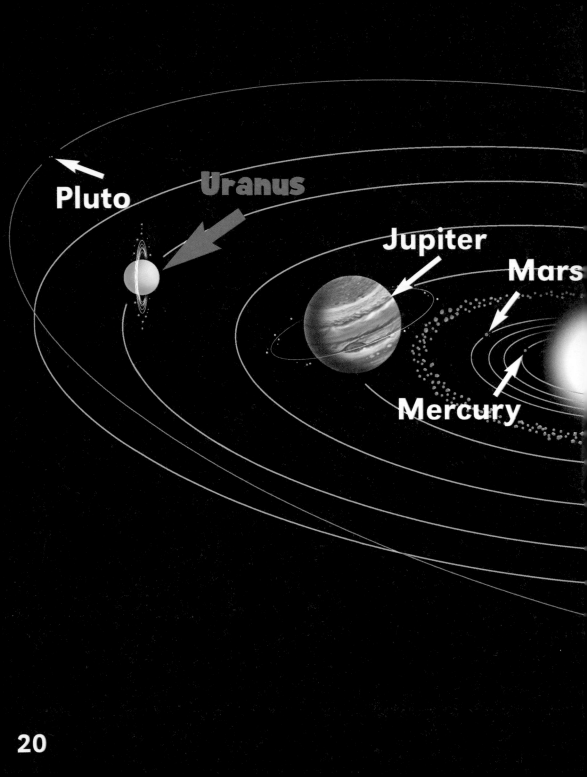

Pluto

Uranus

Jupiter

Mars

Mercury

# URANUS
## IN OUR SOLAR SYSTEM

Sun

Venus

Saturn

Earth

Neptune

# YOUR NEW WORDS

**crater** (**kray**-tur) a large hole in the ground made by a comet or meteorite

**gas giants** (gass **jye**-uhnts) the four largest planets

**orbit** (**or**-bit) the path around an object

**solar system** (**soh**-lur **siss**-tuhm) the group of planets, moons, and other things that travel around the Sun

**Titania** (tuh-**tane**-yuh) Uranus's largest moon

**Uranus** (**yur**-uh-nus) a planet named after the Roman god of the sky

*Voyager 2* (**voi**-ij-uhr 2) the first and only space probe to visit Uranus and Neptune

# Earth and Uranus

A year is how long it takes a planet to go around the Sun.

 **Earth's year =365 days**

**Uranus's year =30,687 Earth days**

A day is how long it takes a planet turn one time.

 **Earth's day = 24 hours**

**Uranus's day = 17 Earth hours**

A moon is an object that circles around a planet.

 **Earth has 1 moon**

**Uranus has at least 27 moons**

**Did you know scientists do not know which way is North on Uranus?**

# INDEX

## FIND OUT MORE
### Book:
*Children's Atlas of the Universe*
By Robert Burnham
Reader's Digest Children's Publishing, Inc., 2000

### Website:
Solar System Exploration
http://sse.jpl.nasa.gov/planets

## MEET THE AUTHOR:

**Christine Taylor-Butler** is the author of more than 20 books for children. She holds a degree in Engineering from M.I.T. She lives in Kansas City with her family, where they have a telescope for searching the skies.